MAMA MIA!
Now That's Italian!

*A tribute to growing up Italian
and the food that impacted my life*

FRANCO PISANI

Bellavita Publishing
Colorado Springs, Colorado

Book Design: Kenneth Guentert, The Publishing Pro, LLC, Colorado Springs, Colorado
Photos: www.bluefoxphotography.com and the Pisani family album.

Bellavita Publishing
2802 W. Colorado Ave.
Colorado Springs, CO 80904
bellavitapublish@aol.com

ISBN-13: 978-1456524869
ISBN-10: 1456524860

Check out Paravicini's Italian Bistro at www.paravicinis.com

Printed in the United States of America.

To Mom and Dad

Thank you for the sacrifices you made to give us what we needed to succeed in life. Mom, I know there were times when you went with out buying yourself a new outfit so that we could go ice-skating. Dad, I know that you didn't want to leave the house at midnight to pick me up from work when I was fifteen, but you did it anyway. Mom and Dad, thank you for bringing your traditions over from Italy and passing them on to us. And thank you for teaching us kids the value of good education and work habits. Mom, your recipes have made me successful, and I will continue to call you with my cooking questions.

Grazie mama e papa per tutti che abbiate fatto ed ancora faccia per noi.

CONTENTS

Chapter One

Baptisms

Relatives Visiting From Italy

If you are Italian, Baptism is the day that you become a good Catholic boy (or girl). If you are a boy, this is the day that your mother starts thinking that you are going to grow up and become a priest (and boy, was my mother wrong!). Anyway, Baptism is the first major event of your life. Your parents choose your godparents, usually close friends, true *paisanos* who will raise you if your parents die, God forbid, while you are young. This is serious business, and much thought goes into picking the right godparents. It is a great honor—and responsibility—to be asked. My parents chose great godparents for me, Connie and Nick Solla.

The day before the christening, cooking begins. All of the aunts and your soon to be godmother make cookies, enough for two years of Girl Scout fundraisers. Your father and uncles go the airport to pick up your relatives from Italy. When they get back to the house, *madone*, here comes the food! You'd think the relatives had been on an eight-week journey on the Andrea-Doria, not an eight-hour plane ride. Back to the food ... a little soup, a little salad, a little pasta, a nice steak or veal dish, and some dessert espresso. Oh yea, and cookies.

MENU
Relatives Visiting from Italy

Minestrone Soup
Fresh Mozzarella and Roasted Pepper Salad
Shrimp Renata
Steak with Portabella
Cannoli

Minestrone Soup

3 Tbsp. olive oil
2 cloves garlic
1 small onion
1 16 oz. can crushed tomatoes
1 small can red kidney beans
1 small can garbanzo beans
2 celery stalks, sliced
2 carrots, sliced
1 zucchini, sliced
1 small head of cabbage, diced or cubed
1 gallon water
salt and pepper
1 lb. cheese tortellini
fresh parmigiana cheese

Sauté onion and garlic in olive oil. Add carrots, celery, zucchini, cabbage, and water. Bring to a boil. Add tomatoes, beans, salt and pepper. Bring to a boil again. Add tortellini. When pasta is cooked serve in a bowl. Grate fresh parmigiana cheese on top and serve.

VISITORS FROM ITALY: When they get back to the house, *madone*, here comes the food! You'd think the relatives had been on an eight-week journey on the Andrea-Doria, not an eight-hour plane ride.

Mozzarella, Tomato, and Roasted Pepper Salad

2 balls fresh mozzarella
2 large beef steak tomatoes
1 small jar roasted red peppers
1 small red onion
2 cloves garlic
3 Tbsp. olive oil
4 leaves fresh chopped basil
   salt and pepper

Slice mozzarella and tomatoes. Set aside. Julienne red onions and peppers, and mix together with garlic, basil, olive oil, salt, and pepper.

Arrange tomato and mozzarella around the rim of the plate. Place pepper salad mixture in the middle. Sprinkle salt and pepper over tomatoes and mozzarella. Drizzle olive oil over the whole plate.

Shrimp Renata

1 bag tortellini pasta
½ lb. diced prosciutto
1 lb. shrimp, peeled
4 c. tomato sauce
½ lb. butter
½ lb. frozen peas
¼ lb. grated parmesan cheese
2 pints heavy cream
½ bunch chopped parsley
   salt and white pepper to taste

In a sauce pan, bring heavy cream to boil. Reduce heat. Add tomato sauce, shrimp. Add prosciutto, peas, and butter. Let reduce. Bring a pot of water to boil and drop in tortellini. Cook five minutes. Drain pasta and add to the sauce. Mix in parmesan cheese, chopped parsley, salt, and pepper.

Steak Portabella

    2 New York Strip Steaks
       flour
       salt
       pepper
       cognac
    2 oz. portabella mushrooms, sliced
    2 oz. heavy cream
    2 Tbsp. butter

Coat steak with flour. Sauté steak until golden brown. Flame with cognac. Add mushrooms, cream, and butter. Reduce and serve.

Cannoli

    1 lb. ricotta impastada cheese
    ¼ lb. chocolate chips
    1 oz. Galliano liqueur
    ½ c. sugar
    4 each cannoli shells
       powdered sugar for garnish

In a bowl, mix ricotta cheese, chocolate chips, Galliano, and sugar. Mix until smooth. Fill a large pastry bag with the filling, and insert filling inside a cannoli shell. Fill both sides of the shell. Arrange cannolis on a plate, and sprinkle with powdered sugar.

ڪڪڪ

The Christening

After dinner, everyone talks about old times and who the baby looks like (it always looks like their favorite relative). Eventually, they go to bed. In the morning, the Broadway production begins—getting the food ready so that everyone can eat as soon as they get back from church. The garage turns into a banquet hall—with a buffet table, folding chairs, and tablecloths in place, and even a bar set up in the corner. Uncle Frank brings over his homemade wine. The whole family pitches in, and they don't miss a thing. Finally, everyone gets dressed and goes off to the church. The ceremony begins. The baby is dressed in a white gown, and it doesn't matter if you are a boy or a girl. Right before the end of the service, one of the aunts goes home to start the food. God forbid that people should arrive and the food is not ready. People arrive home to a full buffet, and everyone oohs and aahs. Then we *mangia*. The baby gets passed around like a football, and everyone fights over who gets to hold the baby the longest and whose turn it is. The kids run off and get into mischief because the adults are having a good time and not really watching. Mom and Dad look at each other and smile. It is their day to be proud.

MENU
The Christening

(buffet style, serves 25 people)
Insalada Italiano
Sausage and Peppers
Oven-roasted Chicken
Roast Beef with Gravy
Italian Rum Cake

Insalada Italiano

1 head iceberg lettuce
1 head romaine lettuce
1 head escarole lettuce
1 head radicchio lettuce
½ c. olive oil
1 Tbsp. garlic
1 Tbsp. red wine vinegar
1 small red onion, diced
¼ lb. provolone cheese, diced
¼ lb. salami, diced
¼ lb. mozzarella cheese, diced
¼ lb. ham, diced

Wash and chop lettuce. Place in a bowl. Add all other ingredients, mix together, and serve.

Italian Sausage and Peppers

2 lbs. Italian sausage links (spicy)
6 sweet red peppers, cut in strips
6 sweet green peppers, cut in strips
2 large onions, cut in strips
1 clove garlic, diced
salt and pepper
2 c. water

Place sausage in the oven and roast at 350 degrees for 15-20 minutes. In a separate pot, sauté peppers, onions, and garlic. Add water and cover until sausage is cooked. Place sausage on a plate and top with pepper mixture.

Oven-Roasted Chicken

    4 chickens, cut up
    ½ c. olive oil
    1 Tbsp. garlic, crushed
    1 Tbsp. red wine vinegar
    1 small red onion, diced
    2 tsp. oregano
    2 tsp. crushed red pepper
       salt and pepper

Mix olive oil, garlic, red wine vinegar, red onion, oregano, crushed red pepper, salt and pepper in a bowl. Place chicken and the mixture in an oven pan and let sit in the refrigerator overnight. Cook in the oven at 350 degrees for one-half hour or until browned and no pink is left inside. Serve.

Roast Beef with Gravy

    1 large top round roast
    4 carrots
    4 stalks celery
    3 large onions
    2 cloves garlic
       salt and pepper
    3 c. water

Place roast beef in a roasting pan. Cover the roast with salt and pepper. Cut up carrots, celery, and onions and add to the pan. Add garlic. Cook in a 350-degree oven until roast reaches 230 degrees. Remove roast from pan and let rest before carving. To make gravy, deglaze roasting pan with water and puree ingredients in a blender. Slice roast and top with gravy.

Italian Rum Cake

Cake:

    4 eggs (jumbo)
    1 c. sugar
    1 c. flour
    1 tsp. cream of tartar
    1 tsp. vanilla
    1 tsp. baking powder
    ¼ c. cold water

Cream sugar with eggs. Add flour and rest of ingredients, one at a time. Spray pans with Pam. Bake at 350 degrees for twenty minutes. Makes three eight-inch layer cake pans.

Syrup:

    1 Tbsp. sugar
    2 c. water
    ½ c. rum
    1 tsp. orange extract

Cream Filling:

    1 qt. milk
    8 egg yolks
    6 Tbsp. flour
    8 Tbsp. sugar

Use whisk to mix in a saucepan on low heat. Stir in one direction only. You can use a double boiler. Add one teaspoon vanilla or rum (For chocolate, use one tablespoon cocoa.)

Ladle syrup onto layers, one layer at a time, adding vanilla filling, then cake, then chocolate filling, then cake.

TAKING A BREAK: The cooks finally get a chance to unwind—and soon show that maybe we've worked them a bit too hard.

Chapter Two
Sunday Dinners

Doing the Dunk

I remember the Sunday mornings of my child-hood as if they were today. By 11 A.M., the house is filled with the smells of garlic, basil, and stewing tomatoes. The scents are hypnotizing, and I am drawn to the tomato sauce as if I were a zombie. The sauce is filled with sausage, meatballs, and *bracciole*. On the counter, there is a fresh loaf of bread from the Como Bakery. The trick is to grab a piece of the bread, dip it in the sauce, and get it into my mouth before being smacked on the hand by a wooden spoon. It rarely works. "Get a dish!" my mother tells me. "Don't dunk the bread in the sauce. I should be raising pigs; they have better manners than my kids." My big brother is behind her back, laughing because he just got away with "the dunk" not five minutes earlier. My mother is only pretending to be angry and hands me a dish of sauce with a piece of bread. It is delicious but not nearly as much fun as doing the dunk.

Sunday Dinner

Sunday dinners, after church, are a big deal. You can drive through the streets of my childhood neighborhood with your windows down and smell the stewing tomatoes. The sauce is not your every day spaghetti sauce. It is special. It is "Sunday gravy." It is loaded with meatballs, fresh sausage, *bracciole*, and sometimes pork chops. There is always a salad or soup and homemade pasta with the meat from the sauce served on the side. My favorite is stuffed shells. There is always another main dish like veal or chicken cutlets, a starch, a vegetable, and Italian pastries for dessert. Oh yea, and cookies. There is always cookies and espresso. Sundays are all about the food. There is so much food, you'd think there are thirty more people coming to dinner. The Sunday table is set with a tablecloth and cloth napkins, never paper napkins. Homemade red wine is served. Even the kids get wine with Pellegrino water so they don't feel left out. It is a great day that always ends with a Sunday nap.

MENU
Sunday Dinner

Salad
Sunday Gravy (Tomato Sauce)
Meatballs
Sausage
Bracciole
Baked Stuffed Shells
Veal Milanese
Oven-roasted Potatoes
Zucchini and Tomatoes
Profiteroles

A BIG DEAL: Sundays are all about food. There
is so much food, you'd think there are thirty
more people coming to dinner.

Tomato Sauce

    ¼ c. olive oil
    2 small onions, sliced
    ¼ lb. fresh basil
    2 cloves garlic, minced
    2 cans crushed tomatoes
       salt and pepper

In a large pot, sauté onions and garlic in olive oil. Add the tomatoes. Bring to a boil. Add meatballs , sausage, and bracciole. Simmer for an hour or so before adding chopped fresh basil. Season with salt and pepper.

Meatballs

    1 lb. ground beef
    2 eggs
    ½ c. bread crumbs
    1 clove garlic, minced
    ¼ c. parmigiana cheese
    ⅓ c. parsley, minced
       salt and pepper

In a large bowl, combine all ingredients. Mix well, shape into balls, and drop into sauce.

Sausage

Find a sausage you like at your local Italian market. Cut into five links, and drop into the sauce.

Bracciole

    4 pieces bottom round steak pounded with a mallet
    ¼ c. olive oil
    1 c. garlic, chopped
    1 c. grated parmigiana cheese
       salt and pepper

Rub garlic into the steak. Sprinkle with cheese and parsley. Roll steak into a log and truss with string. Fry in olive oil until brown , and then simmer in tomato sauce for an hour or until tender.

Cook sauce with all the meats for an hour or so. Then remove meat from sauce and serve on the side. Use sauce for shells.

Baked Stuffed Shells

    1 box large shells
    3 lbs. ricotta cheese
    3 eggs, beaten
    ¼ c. grated cheese
    3 tsp. chopped parsley
       salt and pepper

Boil shells. Set aside and cool. Mix all other ingredients in a bowl with a spoon. Fill shells with mixture and place in a baking dish. Cover shells with sauce and bake at 350 degrees for thirty minutes.

Veal Milanese

    4 4 oz. veal scaloppini
    2 eggs
    1 c. bread crumbs
    2 tsp. chopped parsley
       salt and pepper
    ¼ c. olive oil
    2 Tbsp. butter
    1 lemon
       white wine
    4 slices mozzarella cheese

Mix eggs, parsley, salt, and pepper. Dip veal in egg, then in bread crumbs. Sauté breaded veal on both sides in olive oil. Cover with cheese. Add wine, lemon, and butter. Cover with a lid and simmer until cheese is melted.

Oven-roasted Potatoes

    1 lb. red potatoes
    ¼ c. olive oil
    2 Tbsp. chopped parsley
    2 Tbsp. oregano
       salt and pepper

Boil potatoes. Then cut in half and mix in a bowl with other ingredients. Place potatoes on a sheet pan and roast in a 350-degree oven until golden brown.

THE NEXT GENERATION: "Doing the Dunk" requires grabbing a piece of the bread, dipping it in the sauce, and getting it into your mouth before being smacked on the hand by a wooden spoon. It rarely works.

Zucchini and Tomatoes

    4 zucchini, cut into strips
    4 tomatoes, diced
    1 onion, chopped
    2 garlic cloves, minced
    ⅓ cup olive oil
       salt and pepper

Heat olive oil in a large fry pan heat. Add zucchini and cook till tender. Add tomatoes, chopped onions, garlic, salt, and pepper. Continue cooking for about three minutes.

Profiteroles

    ¼ c. water
    ¼ c. butter
    1/8 tsp. salt
    ½ c. flour
    2 large eggs
       custard filling
       chocolate glaze

Preheat oven to 400 degrees. In a small saucepan, combine water, butter, and salt. Over medium heat, bring to boiling. Remove from heat. Immediately, with wooden spoon, beat in all the flour. Over low heat, beat until mixture leaves sides of pan and forms a ball, one to two minutes. Remove from heat. Add one egg; with portable mixer or wooden spoon, beat until well blended. Add other egg and beat until the dough is shiny and satiny, about one minute. Drop the dough by rounded tablespoons two inches apart onto ungreased cookie sheet. Bake thirty-five to forty minutes or until puffed and golden brown. Puffs should sound hollow when lightly tapped with finger tips.

CHAPTER THREE

Dating

The Big Date Dinner

I can only give you a man's view of what dating was like in an Italian-American family. I bet my sister had a different experience than her two very big older brothers. When I was about sixteen, my friend Carmine and I were dating two girls who were not Italian. They were best friends like Carmine and me. We knew my parents were going out—it must have been their anniversary or something—so me and Carmine planned to invite our girlfriends over and to cook them dinner. A great plan, I thought at the time. After my parents left, I started cooking, Carmine set the table, and it was going great. I got out a bottle of wine, and the table couldn't have looked better. We were even using my Mom's good plates. Then it happened—disaster! My parents came home early. My mother looked at my father and said, "I told you they were up to something!" What could I say? We were busted. Then my father said, "Look, honey. How nice of them to cook us dinner for our anniversary." Then they took out two more place settings and sat down to eat with us. Me and Carmine looked at each other like, "What the hell are we going to do now?"

<u>**MENU**</u>
Franco and Carmine's
(Not So Romantic) Big Date Dinner

Mozzarella en Carozza
Caesar Salad
Paglia E Fieno
Mixed Berries Zabaglione

Mozzarella en Carozza

  6   pieces of whole milk mozzarella cut ¼" thick
12 slices white bread
  4 eggs, beaten
  1 c. flour
  2 Tbsp. chopped parsley
  2 c. bread crumbs
  2 c. olive oil blend
  2 c. tomato sauce

In a sauté pan, heat olive oil. Place cheese between two slices of bread, making a sandwich. Dip cheese sandwich in flour, then eggs, then bread crumbs. Be sure to cover the entire sandwich or it will leak. Place breaded cheese sandwich in hot oil and fry until golden brown. Place on paper towel, pat grease off, and serve over hot tomato sauce.

Caesar Salad

    1 large head of romaine lettuce cut and washed
    1 c. olive oil
    2 cloves garlic
    8 anchovy filets
    1 fresh lemon, juiced
    2 egg yolks
    2 Tbsp. vinegar
    1 Tbsp. Dijon mustard
       salt and pepper
       croutons

In a blender, mix garlic and anchovies. Add mustard and egg yolks. Slowly add olive oil. Mix lemon juice and vinegar together and slowly add them to blender. In a salad bowl, toss lettuce with dressing, top with croutons, and grate cheese over the top.

Paglia E Fieno
(straw and hay)

    1 lb. spinach and egg fettuccini
    ½ lb. diced prosciutto
    ½ lb. butter
    ½ lb. frozen peas
    ¼ c. grated parmesan cheese
    2 pints heavy cream
    ½ bunch chopped parsley
       salt and white pepper to taste

In a sauce pan, heat cream and bring to a boil. Reduce heat. Add prosciutto, peas, and butter. Reduce sauce. Bring a pot of water to a boil, drop in fettuccini, and cook five minutes. Drain the pasta, and add to the sauce. Then mix in cheese, chopped parsley, salt, and pepper.

Mixed Berries Zabaglione

    6 egg yolks
    ½ c. sugar
    2 oz. marsala wine
    1 lb. mixed seasonal berries

Mix egg yolks and sugar with a wire whip in a bowl, then cook in a double boiler. Whisk until eggs are frothy. Stir in the wine and continue to whisk. Let cool. Serve warm over berries.

ɔɔɔ

The Matchmaking Meal

I had another friend named Anthony. One day when we were about eighteen, his Mom was out of town. Anthony wanted to impress his girlfriend, and what better way than to fix her a romantic dinner for two. The problem was that he didn't know how to cook. Here comes Franco to the rescue. Anthony set the table with candles, wine, and the whole bit while I hid in the kitchen and cooked his meal. It was a great one, even if I do say so myself. We pulled it off, and he ended up marrying the girl. I wonder if she knows he didn't cook her that romantic meal. (She will after she reads this).

MENU
The Meal that Got Anthony's Wife to Love Him

Chicken Saltimbocca
Green Beans with Almonds
Fried Peppers and Potatoes
Strawberries Romanoff

Chicken Saltimbocca

- 4 pieces chicken scaloppini
- 4 leaves fresh sage
- 2 c. mushrooms sliced
- 1 c. white wine
- 2 c. brown sauce
- 8 oz. thin sliced prosciutto
  - pieces mozzarella cheese

Tenderize and flour chicken. Sauté chicken in olive oil. Add mushrooms and wine. Put prosciutto, sage, and cheese on chicken. To finish sauce, add brown gravy to pan.

Brown Sauce

- 2 lbs. veal bones
- 1 large carrot, peeled and diced
- 1 large onion, peeled and diced
- 6 cloves of garlic
- 1 small can of tomato paste
- 2 stalks of celery, diced
- 1 Tbsp. whole black peppercorns
- 2 bay leaves
- 1 small bunch fresh thyme
- 2 qts. cold water

1) Heat oven to 350 degrees. Place veal bones in a roasting pan, and rub with tomato paste. 2) Roast in oven until brown. 3) Transfer bones to a large stockpot. Add all remaining ingredients. Bring to a boil; then reduce heat and simmer for two hours. 4) Strain stock in a cheesecloth-lined colander and cool. Place in small containers and freeze.

Green Beans Almondine

    1 lb. blanched green beans
    1 fresh lemon
    1 Tbsp. butter
    ¼ c. white wine
    ¼ c. toasted almonds
      salt and pepper

Sauté blanched beans. Add wine, lemon, and butter to make a sauce. Top with salt, pepper, and toasted almonds.

Fried Peppers and Potatoes

    5 potatoes, peeled and cut into round slices
    5 peppers (mixed red and green), sliced
    3 fresh tomatoes, chopped
    ¼ c. olive oil
    1 tsp. oregano
      salt and pepper

Combine oil and potatoes; fry for ten minutes. Add peppers and fry for fifteen minutes. When potatoes and peppers are three-quarters cooked, add tomatoes and fry for five minutes more. Add salt, pepper, and oregano. Serve.

Strawberries Romanov

    1 lb. fresh strawberries
    2 c. flavored whipped cream
    2 oz. grande marnier
    ½ c. sugar
      chocolate for shaving

Cut up strawberries, and soak in grande marnier. Add sugar. Fold in the whipped cream. Spoon into a large glass. Shave chocolate over the top.

ès ès ès

The Franco Frittata

The "Franco Frittata" was my way of getting invited back to a girl's place. It started in college. I would get to know a girl and at the end of the night, I would ask her if I could go back to her place and make her a Franco Frittata. "What's a Franco Frittata?" she would ask. "Well, if you have eggs," I would say, "I can make it with anything else you have in your fridge." It's an Italian omelet. Once I got into her kitchen, I would go to work taking out all the stuff in her fridge and making this Franco Frittata. The very first time I did this, the girl says to me, "There is nothing sexier then watching a man cook in my kitchen." After that, I made it a common practice to coerce girls into letting me make them a Franco Frittata.

The Infamous Franco Frittata

    3 oz. sliced prosciutto
    2 Tbsp. olive oil
    ¼ lb. spinach, chopped
    ¼ lb. cheese
    4 eggs, beaten
    1 c. cooked potatoes, diced

In a non-stick pan, sauté prosciutto in olive oil. Add spinach and potatoes. Then add eggs, and cook until firm. Flip. Add cheese. Serve hot.

CHAPTER FOUR

Italian Neighborhoods

Mount Carmel Feast

The city I grew up in was very segregated. Almost every nationality had its own neighborhood. I lived in Town Plot, a small Italian neighborhood where most everyone knew everybody else. Our church was Our Lady of Mount Carmel, which had an Italian feast every year. We couldn't wait for it. All the old church ladies made the sauce for the fried dough. Hmm, I wonder how that ever worked out— every one thinks that their tomato sauce is better then everyone else's! Anyway, the fried dough with tomato sauce was the best. Then there was pizza, sausage and peppers Grinders, Italian pastries—I'm getting teary-eyed just thinking about it. And let's not forget about the *suffritto*, an Italian stew made with veal hearts, then served on a grinder roll. Mmm! There were great Italian-American bands playing with the old people dancing all night. The younger guys played a game of *morra* (an Italian number game). It was a great time in the neighborhood.

Menu
Mt. Carmel Feast

Fried dough
Soffritto
Sausage and Peppers

Fried dough

4 pieces pizza dough
2 c. tomato sauce
1 qt. vegetable oil
   grated parmesan cheese

The Dough:

4 c. flour
2 tsp. salt
2 oz. yeast
1 c. water

In a two-quart stainless steel mixing bowl, mix all dough ingredients. Cover with a cloth and let sit for one hour. Flatten dough and allow to rise another thirty minutes. Cut into four pieces. Roll the dough flat. Fry the dough in oil until it is golden brown on both sides. Top with tomato sauce and cheese.

THE BROTHERS PISANI: Thanks, Joe, for the Suffrito recipe.

Suffritto

    5 lbs. veal hearts
    2 onions
    3 green bell peppers
    3 cloves garlic, chopped
       olive oil
    1 can crushed tomatoes
       salt
       black pepper
    3 Tbsp. crushed red pepper flakes

Parboil veal hearts until blood is no longer visible. Cut hearts in half. Clean hearts, removing fat and nerves. Cut into half-inch dice. Chop equal amounts onion and pepper into half-inch dice. Brown veal, onions, pepper, and garlic in olive oil. Add crushed tomatoes, salt, black pepper, and red pepper to taste. Bring to boil, reduce heat, and simmer for 1½ to 2 hours.

Sausage and Peppers Grinder

    2 lbs. Italian sausage links (spicy)
    6 sweet red peppers, cut in strips
    6 sweet green peppers, cut in strips
    2 large onions, cut in strips
    1 clove garlic diced
       salt and pepper
    2 c. water
    4 grinder rolls

Cut sausage into strips and cook in a sauté pan. Add peppers, onions, and garlic. When sausages are cooked, add water and cover. Simmer for about three minutes. Serve on a grinder roll or Italian bread.

෨෭෨෭෨෭

Great Grinders

Another great neighborhood staple was the "grinder" (or "sub," depending on who you asked). Every one had a favorite. Mine was Zappone's. My brother loved Zappone grinders so much he married Nick Zappone's daughter, Mary Jean. I tried to get the other daughter, Diane, but it didn't work out. D'amelio's Joey & Johnny made great grinders. Mark, Angelo and Mikie from Napoli's had awesome grinders, too. I had a part-time after school job at Napoli's. I ate so many of their grinders that I ended up owing them money on payday. Avventura's is making great grinders to this day. It took a lot of begging and groveling, but my sister-in-law finally gave me a recipe for a Zappone grinder.

Zappone Grinder
Italian Combo

- ½ loaf of Italian bread, sliced down the middle with some of the inside removed
- 3 slices Krakus imported ham
- 3 slices Carondo hot cappicola
- 3 slices Dilusso Genoa salami
- 3 slices mild provolone cheese
- shredded iceberg lettuce
- sliced tomato
- Hellman's mayonaise
- Frank's Red Hot Sauce

Optional
- sliced hot cherry peppers
- oil and vinegar
- salt and pepper

CHAPTER FIVE
Meeting the Family

The Father from the Old Country

I am sitting here with a grin on my face as I write this chapter, thinking about the torture involved for a young person meeting an Italian family. It never mattered whether my girl friend was meeting my family or whether I was meeting hers. Right after high school, I was dating this girl, and it was time to meet her family. The minute I walked into her house, her Dad gives me a look of stone. Her Mom is in the kitchen cooking. My girl friend, her dad, and I take seats at the dining-room table. But the Dad immediately sends my girl friend off to help the Mom with the cooking. It's time for guy talk. He hands me a glass of homemade wine, some cheese, some home-made *soppressata*, and a nice antipasto. Anyway, here it comes. "So you and my daughter like each other, no?"

"Oh, yes, sir. We do."

"You love her," he says, shaking his head.

"Yea, I think I do.

Now some people come to America but never leave the old country. In Italian, he says to me, "So, Franco, when do you bring your parents over?"

"Well, sir, I don't know. Why?"

Now here it comes and it hits me so hard I feel like I've just gone ten rounds with Rocky Marciano. "Well, so you can talk to the priest," he says. "You two should geta married."

And this after only four dates. I almost choke on the freakin' provolone. Then the girls come out with the food, and the discussion stops. We sit down, eat some food, make some small talk in Italian. The sweat is dripping from my forehead, and it's not from the hot peppers either. We finish eating the main meal, and the girls clear the table and bring the dessert, the espresso, the Sambuca, and the cookies. The Dad and I continue our conversation.

"Well, sir. I don't think I'm ready for marriage," I say. "I think I'd like to go to college."

"Then why you wasta my time and my daughters time," he says. "Tomorrow I talk to your Mom and Dad, and we see whata they gonna say."

Thank God my parents were not into arranged marriages. They told the guy there would be no trading of sheep and goats ... this was not the old country ... if the kids do not want to get married, then they don't want to get married ... if they do, then *buona fortuna* ... who are we to force them.

Well, that ended the dating between me and this girl, not to mention that fact that two weeks later her Dad tried to run me over with his car.

LA FAMIGLIA: How would you like to meet this family? And these are just the cousins from one side.

<u>**MENU**</u>
The Dinner that Gave Me Heartburn

Antipasto
Pasta Bolognese
Veal Parmigiana
Baba al Rhum

Italian Antipasto

    10 slices prosciutto
    10 slices capicollo
    10 slices imported boiled ham
    10 slices provolone
    10 slices pieces pickled cauliflower
     1 c. pickled mushrooms
     1 c. pickled eggplant
     2 slices roasted pepper
    10 pepperoncini
     1 small can chickpeas
    ½ head iceberg lettuce

Slice lettuce and arrange on an oval platter. Place all pickled ingredients in the middle of the platter. Roll all meats and cheese and slice three times. Arrange on top of lettuce. Slice and arrange roasted peppers. Add chickpeas and olives. Serve cold.

Pasta Bolognese

    1 lb. ground beef
    1 onion, finely chopped
    1 clove garlic, minced
    ¼ c. celery, finely chopped
    2 carrots, finely chopped or grated
    3 leaves basil
    ⅓ c. fresh parsley, chopped
       grated cheese
    3 cans crushed tomatoes
       salt and pepper to taste

In a saucepan, combine oil, garlic, onion, carrots, and celery. Sauté until vegetables are tender. Crumble beef and cook until brown. Add tomatoes and basil. Bring to a boil. Reduce heat and simmer for approximately twenty minutes. Serve over pasta.

Veal Parmigiana

    1 4 oz. veal scaloppini
    2 eggs, beaten
    ½ c. bread crumbs
       olive oil
    4 slices mozzarella cheese
    4 oz. tomato sauce

Dip veal in egg and bread crumbs. Sauté in olive oil. Cover with tomato sauce and cheese. Bake in oven until cheese is browned.

Baba al Rhum

    1 c. shortening
    1 c. sugar
    5 jumbo eggs
    8 eggs
    7 c. flour
    ½ oz. yeast

Mix shortening, sugar, and five eggs. Continue to beat. Add eight more eggs, one at a time. Add flour and yeast until batter looks like elastic. Spray tins. Fill each tin half full. Let rise to top for thirty minutes, then bake at 350 degrees for twenty to twenty-five minutes.

Syrup

    6 c. water
    1 c. sugar
    1 bottle imitation rum
    2 c. light colored rum
      cherries

Bring water, sugar, flavoring, and rum to a boil. Put babas in liquid and soak for a few minutes. Cut "V" and fill with Italian cream. Place cherry on top.

≈≈≈

The Embarrassing Dinner

One day I came home from a date with a couple of hickeys (It's what we did when we were young). My Mom sees them and asks, "What, you're now dating vampires?" I pay no attention and try to ignore her. My first mistake. Then the girl I was dating comes to pick me up because my car is broken. The family was eating dinner when she comes in.

"Would you like to eat with us," my Mom asks.

"No, no, thank you."

But my Dad makes her sit down, and here comes a big steaming plate of pasta, which my Mom sets down right in front of my girl friend. "Eat, eat, honey," Mom says. "That way you don't have to eata my son's neck later."

OH, MY GOD, I WAS SO EMBARRASSED. I can't believe she said that. Well, yes I can. And she doesn't even stop. "What's the matter? Your Mom doesn't fed you before you go out? You have to chew on my poor son's neck!"

"Enough, Mom," I say.

The poor girl just stares at her plate, but she eats her pasta.

MENU
My Mom's Embarrassing Dinner

Spaghetti with Broccoli, Garlic, and Oil
Moma Pisani's Steak Cooked in Beer

Spaghetti with Broccoli, Garlic, and Oil

    1 lb. cooked pasta
    ½ lb. broccoli florets, blanched
    6 garlic cloves, chopped
    ¼ c. olive oil
    3 Tbsp. grated cheese
       salt and pepper

Sauté garlic in olive oil. Add broccoli. Add cooked pasta, cheese, salt and pepper.

Mama Pisani's Steak Cooked in Beer

    2 8 oz. top sirloin steaks
    2 small onions
    1 clove garlic
    ⅓ cup olive oil
       salt and pepper
    1 12 oz. can of beer
    4 leaves basil

Sauté steak in olive oil. Add sliced onions and chopped garlic. Add beer and simmer until steak is tender. Add chopped basil. Add salt and pepper.

CHAPTER SIX
Holidays

There are many Italian-American holiday traditions, but every holiday you can bet your life that two of the relatives will get into an argument. This may be a meaningless argument about what car is better, the Lincoln or the Caddie, with another uncle chiming in that the Buick is better than both. Or it may be about who is better looking, Sophia Loren or Gina Lollabrigida. Anyway, in an Italian argument, everyone has to talk louder than the next person and the hands have to fly around like mad. The hand gestures are so forceful that if you put a flashlight in each hand, you risk having a 747 landing right in your living room. Eventually, one of the aunts comes into the room and tells everyone to shut up. Then things settle down.

Recipe for an Italian Argument

    2 Calabrese Italians (Calabrese Italians work better because they are known as thick heads)
    1 gal. home-made wine
    1 topic of discussion on which the two parties do not agree

Have the two Italians drink the wine. Ask their opinion on the above topic. Let the yelling begin.

No *Zeppoles* for You

Italians celebrate the Feast of St. Joseph on March 19th. This is a day to give thanks for all of your answered prayers. Food is the focus of the day, even though all of the dishes are meatless because the feast falls during Lent. The most memorable dish is the St. Joseph's Day *zeppole*. I would describe it as a cruller filled with either sweet ricotta, chocolate, or vanilla pastry cream. We were lucky because as kids we had a Joseph in the family. Then again, what Italian family didn't have a Joseph or a Giuseppe in their family?

After dinner one year, my Mom was finishing the *zeppoles* and told me and my brother to go and play, that the *zeppoles* will be done in a half-hour. So we go out to meet up with a couple of our friends, and we decide to get into a little trouble. We liked to play this game where we run through the neighbors' yards and rip clothes off the clothes line. It seemed funny at the time—don't ask me why. Anyway we rip the clothes off the line, run into the street, start throwing clothes at each other, and there is my Dad staring at us. Me and my brother freeze. My Dad doesn't have to say much. He just points to the house and says, "Home! Now!" We go home with fear in our hearts, expecting a beating, but it is much worse than that. We get sent to our rooms without *zeppoles*. You can imagine the torture because the whole house smells like *zeppoles*. Then, after two hours, we hear a knock on the door. It is our soft-hearted Mom, with two glasses of milk and two *zeppoles*. Of course, we have to thank St. Joseph for answering our prayer:

THE ITALIAN FEAST: Even if all the dishes are meatless, food is the focus of the day.

"Please, St. Joseph, don't let us go to bed with no *zeppoles*."

St. Joseph's Zeppoles

    2 c. shortening
    4 c. water
       pinch of salt
    4 c. flour
    1 tsp. baker's ammonia
    4 c. eggs (about 13 jumbo)
       custard filling
       oil for frying pan

Boil shortening, water, and salt in pan over stove. When melted, add flour to water and stir. Dough will end up looking like cream-puff dough. Place cooked dough into mixer. Add baker's ammonia and continue to mix well. Add eggs, one at a time. When dough is thoroughly mixed, place in a pastry bag with a star tip. In the meantime, place a deep frying pan with oil on stove. Place wax paper or parchment paper in oil and remove. With pastry bag, make one round of circles on paper. Make about six circles and place wax paper and circles of dough in frying pan. Hold down zeppole with a screen or something so that they remain in the hot oil. When they start to separate from paper, remove paper and turn zeppole over; continue to hold them down in the oil. When all zeppole are cooked, slit in half and place custard filling inside. Place small amount in center with cherry. Sprinkle with confectioner's sugar.

                        ✿✿✿

Easter Sunday

Man, there are so many things leading up to Easter—Easter suits for the boys, Easter dresses and bonnets for the girls, and Easter pictures. On Palm Sunday, we go to Mass and get palms and come home for a big dinner. Someone always makes a cross out of the palms so you can hang it in your room. Then on Good Friday, we have a meatless dinner. Finally, on Easter Sunday, the Easter bunny comes and brings each of us a giant egg with a toy inside. Mm-mm, I loved those eggs. I mean, they were gigantic—one or two feet tall. But we can not have any chocolate before church. We get all dressed up, go to church, and then come home and eat all kinds of special Easter food. There are Easter pies— not apple or blueberry but pies stuffed with Italian cured meats and cheeses. And there are Easter breads shaped like baskets with eggs in them. No wonder I was a fat kid. And of course there are cookies. The, finally, the whole family gets together to see what each of us got in our Italian chocolate egg.

MENU
Easter Traditions

Easter Bread
Pizza Piena
Ricotta Pie
Rice Pie

Easter Bread

    10 c. flour
     4 oz. yeast cake
    ½ c. warm water
     1 c. sugar
     1 c. Crisco
    12 eggs, beaten
    ½ c. milk
     2 tsp. orange flavor
     1 tsp. salt

Combine all ingredients to form dough. Knead dough well. Cover and let rise for three hours. Shape into loaves. Let rise and additional two hours. Brush with a little reserved egg and bake in a 325-degree oven for approximately one hour.

Pizza Piena

Dough

     4 c. flour
    ½ c. oil
     2 tsp. salt
     3 eggs
       water

Filling

     3 lb. ricotta
    12 eggs, beaten
    ½ lb. chopped prozzutina
    ½ lb. chopped prozzutta
     1 stick chopped pepperoni
     1 basket cheese (pt.)
    1½ balls mozzarella, chopped
     3 Tbsp. grated cheese

Make dough. Roll out like pie crust. Put into ten-inch plates. Pour in filling.

Ricotta Pie

Dough

- 3 eggs, beaten
- 3 c. flour
- ½ c. oil
- ¾ c. sugar
- 1 tsp. baking powder
- ½ c. milk

Mix all ingredients. Roll into ten-inch plates. Makes three pies.

Filling

- 3 lb. ricotta
- 2 c. sugar
- 1 stick unsalted butter, softened
- 1 pt. heavy cream
  - skin of small orange, ground up
- 10 eggs, beaten
- 2 tsp. vanilla

Rice Pie: Boil one-fourth cup rice and drain; add to filling (no orange rind)

Wheat Pie: Add one-half cup wheat berries, boiled and drained, and one-fourth cup candied fruit (no orange rind).

Bake at 325 degrees for twenty-five to thirty minutes. Check like custard pie with a knife.

Christmas Eve

On Christmas Eve, my family always ate a seafood dinner in honor of the "feast of seven fishes." Then we go to Aunt Rose's house for coffee and dessert. There are so many people there, it looks like Aunt Rose's house is bursting at the seams. The women gather in one room, the men in the other, for loud discussions. Right before midnight, the newest member of the family gets to put the Baby Jesus in the manger because it was his birthday. Then we all go to Mount Carmel Church for Midnight Mass. Half the kids fall asleep. Then we come home and open presents. Funny, we were all tired in church for Mass but not at home for opening presents. Finally, we go to bed and don't get up to 11 AM, when Mom has a big meal waiting for us. Then we all truck up to George's house for coffee, cookies, desserts, and arguments.

⋨⋩⋨⋩⋨⋩

Different families have different traditions some do thirteen fishes, some do nine, and others do seven. This is more a southern Italian tradition than a northern Italian one. Each number of fishes has different significance. There is no set menu for the feast of the seven fishes but in our house the dishes were traditionally the following:

ON CHRISTMAS EVE: We always go to Aunt Rose's house for coffee and dessert. There are so many people there, it looks like the house is bursting at the seams.

MENU
Feast of the Seven Fishes

Insalada di Mare
A cold seafood salad with scungili, calamari, clams, shrimp, and mussels

Fried Seafood Platter
With smelts, calamari, and shrimp

Zuppa di Pesci
Scungili, calamari, clams, shrimp, mussels, and lobster over pasta al dente

Pasta with Tuna
Shell pasta with canned tuna and sun-dried tomatoes

Baccala
Dry salt cod in a tomato olive sauce

Baked Stuffed Shrimp
Jumbo shrimp with crab meat stuffing

Stuffed Filet of Sole
Baked stuffed sole with shrimp and scallop stuffing

Of course we would always end with cookies, pastries, and other sweets—and fruits and nuts. Pomegranates were always a Christmas Eve treat. Just ask Joe Laccone. One Christmas—I think it was his first time meeting the family—he had a nice white suit on. Me and my other cousins were flicking pomegranate seeds at him. After dinner, his suit looked like it had chicken pocks. Don't forget the espresso and sambucca. Then sit back and enjoy the arguments.

CHAPTER SEVEN

Italian Weddings

Backyards to Banquet Halls

Italian weddings are a Broadway production without the Tony awards, even though five will get you ten there will be a "Tony" at the wedding. If it's your wedding and you're older than thirty, you'll hear your entire family sigh with relief. Thank God, you found someone and are finally getting married. If you're not married by thirty, God forbid, there must be something wrong with you. But you're getting married, and it's a big deal. Your wedding might cost tens of thousands of dollars. That's why Italians don't believe in divorce. The father of the bride wants his money's worth—so your marriage better last longer than a year. If you're the groom, look out for ex-girlfriends trying to run you over on the big day. It's been known to happen. Anyway, wedding planning starts with an enormous invitation list that may include only ten people known to the bride and groom. Italian parents have a mental list of whose weddings they were invited to in the last 20 years and how much they put in the envelope, and they are duty-bound to reciprocate. Once the 200 or so attendees have been decided upon, the nightmare begins.

Who sits with whom and at what table. Italians like to hold grudges—it's a national sport—so you can't sit some people together without starting a war. Close family friends and relatives must sit up front. Then you need to pick a gift for everyone, a useless knick-knack with your wedding date on it. Then you have to order special napkins, again with the names of the bride and groom, as if people don't know who's wedding they are at or what day it is. The cake has to look like the Vatican, complete with fountains, columns, stairways, bridges, and statues. Modern Italian wedding cakes require a blueprint more than a recipe. Of course, it wasn't always this way. In the old days, weddings were held in back yards or in church basements—not in million-dollar banquet halls that mimic grand Italian villas. The women of both families would get together and cook the meal. The menus were informal but great tasting. Just look at the movie, The Godfather. The Corleones were a wealthy and powerful family, but they had Connie's wedding in the back yard.

MENU
An Old-Country Wedding

Wedding Soup
Potato Zucchini and Green Bean Salad
Pasta ala Pesto
Chicken Cacciatore
Veal Tuscano
Cookies (See Chapter Nine)
Cherry Nut Wedding Cake (Go to your local bakery)

THE ITALIAN WEDDING

If it's your wedding
and you're older than thirty,
you'll hear your entire family sigh with relief.

Wedding Soup

½ lb. ground beef
¼ c. seasoned bread crumbs
1 egg, beaten
1 Tbsp. chopped parsley
 salt and pepper to taste
1 whole chicken, cut up (8 pieces)
4 c. water
2 c. spinach leaves, cut in pieces
1 small box orzo
¼ c. grated romano cheese

Combine the ground beef, breadcrumbs, egg, parsley, salt, and pepper in a bowl. Mix well and form into tiny meatballs. Meanwhile add chicken to water, cover and boil for five minutes. Add the meatballs to the hot broth and bring to a simmer. Cook for one hour. Remove chicken and peel from the bone. Add orzo and cook for five minutes. Add spinach and peeled chicken. Stir in the cheese and serve immediately.

Potato, Zucchini and Green Bean Salad

1 lb. string beans
3 small green zucchini
4 large potatoes
¼ c. olive oil
 salt and pepper to taste
 pinch of fennel seed

Peel potatoes. Cut into large chunks and boil until tender. Cut zucchini into large chunks and boil with string beans until tender. Strain all ingredients well. Combine string beans, potatoes, and zucchini with oil, salt, pepper, and fennel.

ITALIAN ARCHITECTURE: The cake has to look like the Vatican, complete with fountains, columns, stairways, bridges, and statues.

Pasta ala Pesto

        1 lb. fresh basil leaves
        2 Tbsp. pine nuts
        2 cloves garlic
        1 c. olive oil
        4 Tbsp. grated romano cheese
           salt and pepper
        1 lb. thin spaghetti
        2 Tbsp. butter
        ¼ c. cream

Place basil, pine nuts, and garlic in the blender or food processor. With the motor running, drizzle in the olive oil until it is a smooth puree. Stir in the cheese, and season with salt and pepper. Cook pasta in boiling water. Drain and return to the pot. Add pesto, cream, and butter.

Chicken Cacciatore

        4 chicken legs
        4 chicken thighs
        1 onion, chopped
        1 clove garlic, minced
        ½ c. white wine
        6 basil leaves, chopped
        2 cans crushed tomatoes
        ¼ c. olive oil
        1 c. water
           salt and pepper to taste

In a saucepan, combine oil, garlic, onion, and chicken. Fry until chicken is browned. Add wine and sauté for five minutes. Add tomatoes, basil, salt, and pepper. Simmer over low heat for ten minutes. Add water and simmer over low heat for approximately one hour until chicken starts falling off the bone. Serve over pasta.

THE WAY WE WERE: In the old days, weddings were held in backyards or basements—not in million-dollar banquet halls that mimic grand Italian villas.

CHAPTER EIGHT

Great Recipes I ~~Stole~~ Borrowed from Great Restaurants

Making My Move

One of my first restaurant jobs was at D'luca Pasta. The restaurant bought bread from my mother's bakery, and my parents got me a job there as a dishwasher. One day the pizza cook called in sick, and the chef was upset because he didn't know who would make pizza that night. My mom had taught me how to make pizza when I was young, so I made my move. I asked the chef if I could make my own lunch. He said, "Sure." I went to the pizza station, spun the dough and flipped it in the air, added the sauce and cheese, slid the pie into the brick oven, and shut the door. It was a perfect pie (though I must tell you it is not easy getting a pie off the wood pile). The chef asked me if I would like to make pizza, and that's how I became a line cook. D'Luca Pasta is where I got the recipe for Tortellini Carbonara.

Tortellini Carbonara

> 1 bag tortellini pasta
> ½ lb. diced prosciutto
> ½ lb. butter
> ½ lb. frozen peas
> ¼ c. grated parmesan cheese
> 2 pints heavy cream
> ½ bunch chopped parsley
>   salt and white pepper to taste

In a sauce pan, heat cream and bring to a boil. Reduce heat. Add prosciutto, peas, and butter. Reduce the sauce. Bring a pot of water to a boil, drop in tortellini, and cook five minutes. Drain the pasta, and add to the sauce. Then mix in cheese, chopped parsley, salt, and pepper.

ôôô

"Aw, Shucks, I'm Fired"

In high school I hooked up with my best friend, Val, who got me a job at his uncle's restaurant, San Marino, working at the appetizer station. One of my jobs was to shuck the clams. I swear we sold hundreds of clams casino each day, and each clam had to be shucked by hand, which was a long and tedious job, not to mention hard on the manicure. Val also got me fired from this restaurant. We were getting the windows tinted on his car when time got away from us. I told him, "Val I have to go to work."

"Don't worry about it," he said, "I'll talk to Tony." His cousin, Tony, was the restaurant manager.

Well, I was twenty minutes late when I walked in and Tony says, "Franco, go home, you're fired." I told him I was with Val, but Ray said, "Forgetaboutit. Go

MOE BETTER COOKING: Moe Allegrini taught me to ignore the trends and give my customers the best Italian food I can.

home." Anyway, this is where I got the got the recipe for Clams Casino

Clams Casino

    12 cherrystone clams
     2 c. breadcrumbs
     1 tsp. chopped parsley
     1 large green pepper
     1 large red pepper
     3 cloves garlic
    ¼   lb. butter
     4 slices bacon

Shuck clams in half and place to the side. In a food processor, finely chop peppers and garlic. Add breadcrumbs, butter, and parsley. Place topping over the clams. Cut each strip of bacon in threes, and place a piece of bacon on each stuffed clam. Bake in a 350-degree oven till bacon is crisp and clams are golden, about fifteen minutes.

శ్రీశ్రీశ్రీ

So Sous Me

Then I got a chance to work for Chef Don Gordon as his line chef at the Sheraton Waterbury. Later he brought me with him to work as sous chef at the Bridgeport Hilton. He taught me a lot about creating recipes. "Don't be afraid to try things," he said. "The worst thing that can happen is that it will be disgusting, but you might also create a great dish." I got the recipe for Chicken Janette from him.

Chicken Jannette

2 6 oz. chicken breasts, pounded
   flour
   olive oil
   splash white wine
1 tsp. Dijon mustard
¼ c. cream
6 shrimp 16/20 size
2 Tbsp. butter
   pinch of fresh dill
¼ lb. cooked long pasta

In a sauté pan, heat olive oil. Dip the chicken in flour, place in a hot pan, and sauté until golden brown. Add shrimp. When shrimp are pink, add white wine, mustard, and cream. Then add butter and dill, and reduce the sauce. Serve over pasta.

ॐॐॐ

If It Ain't Broke …

The highlight of my early culinary career was working at the 1249 West. Moe Allegrini was a great restaurateur who taught me that "If it ain't broke, don't fix it." By then, the 1249 had been using the same recipes handed down by chef Aldo sixteen years earlier. Here I was, a young up and comer who wanted to change them all. Moe was having none of it. He would yell at me if the fried mozzarella came out a little too dark or if I tried to stack the food in a certain way because that was the trend. The greatest thing Moe taught me, and I apply this in my restaurant today, is to ignore the trends and to give my guests the best Italian food that I can. Don't change the recipes that our elders handed down. Thank you, Moe, for all of your wisdom. The 1249 West is where I learned the right way to make my favorite dish and, veal osso bucco, and, of course, the fried mozzarella.

Veal Osso Bucco

- 6 veal shanks
- 1 c. flour
- ¼ c. olive oil
- 4 each carrots, chopped
- 4 stalks celery, chopped
- 2 small onions, chopped
- ¼ c. red wine
- 6 cloves garlic, chopped
- 1 gal. veal stock
- 1 small can crushed tomatoes
- 1 each roasted red peppers
- ½ c. frozen peas
  fusilli (springs) pasta

Dip veal shanks in flour and sauté in olive oil until golden brown. Remove the veal shanks from the pan and set in a baking dish. Brown carrots, onions, celery, and garlic in the pan. When vegetables are browned, add red wine and deglaze the pan. Pour the vegetable mix over the veal, now in the baking pan. Add veal stock and tomatoes. Cover and bake at 350 degrees for four hours. Place cooked pasta in a serving dish, add shanks to top, cover with sauce, and sprinkle with roasted peppers and peas.

Golden-Brown Fried Mozzarella

 6 pieces of whole milk mozzarella, cut ¼" thick and
   4" long × 2" wide
 4 eggs, beaten
 1 c. flour
   parsley
 2 c. breadcrumbs
 2 c. of olive oil blend
 2 c. tomato sauce

In a sauté pan, heat olive oil. Dip cheese in flour, then eggs, then breadcrumbs and parsley. Be sure to cover the entire piece of cheese or it will leak. Place cheese in hot oil and fry until golden brown ("Not white golden brown, not black golden brown," as my old boss used to say, "GOLDEN BROWN!") Place on paper towel, pat grease off, and serve over hot tomato sauce.

CHAPTER NINE
It's All about the Cookies

You Gotta Have Cookies

While reading this book, you might have noticed that cookies are mentioned in almost every chapter. Well, my mother and her sisters are cookie machines. They would put the Keebler elves to shame. At large events like weddings and baptisms, you'd always find trays with hundreds of cookies on them. My family had a crystal dish with a silver dome, and you could always find cookies underneath. If company came to the house, poof! Out of nowhere cookies would appear. Here are thirty-five cookie recipes, all from my mother. Enjoy.

Batter Cookies

    4 oz. sugar
    1 oz. Crisco
    1 tsp. salt
    ½ c. egg whites
    ½ c. milk
    14 oz. cake flour
    2 oz. flour
    3 tsp. vanilla
    2 tsp. food coloring of your choice

Cream together sugar, Crisco, and salt. Add eggs and milk. Add flour, vanilla, and food color. Beat until batter is creamy. Place batter in a pastry bag and use desired tip to make cookies. Bake in a 350-degree oven for ten minutes.

Sfringi

    1 c. wine (white or red)
    1 tsp. oil
    1 c. water
    1 Tbsp. salt
    4 c. flour
    4 oz. yeast cake

Mix all ingredients well. Let rest for ten minutes. Roll dough into long strips and cut into three-inch pieces. Roll across a hair pick and fry. Can be served plain or with honey.

Angel Wings

    6 eggs
    2 serving spoons oil
    2 serving spoons sugar
    1 tsp. baking powder
    3 c. flour (and extra flour to work with)

Mix the preceding ingredients and let dough rest a while. Roll dough out with macaroni machine. Use one and two setting up to five. Fry in hot oil.

COOKIE-MAKING MACHINES: My mother and her sisters would put the Keebler elves to shame.

Pignoli Cookies

    2 lb. almond paste
    4 c. sugar
    8 egg whites
    2 lb. pignoli

With mixer at medium speed, mix almond paste, sugar, and egg whites. When thoroughly mixed, place dough in a large pastry bag. Place pignoli nuts on cookie sheet. With no tip on pastry bag, squeeze out two-inch lengths of dough onto pignoli nuts. Roll the dough in the nuts and then place on parchment paper covered cookie sheet. Bake at 375 degrees for twenty minutes or until slightly browned. Makes 100 cookies.

Filled Cookies

    6 eggs
    1 c. sugar
    1 c. oil
    6 tsp. baking powder
    1 tsp. lemon extract
    5 c. flour plus 1 c. to roll out dough
       grape jam
       black and white raisins, chopped
       nuts, chopped
       ground cloves
       ground cinnamon

Mix eggs, sugar, oil, water, baking powder, and lemon extract. Add flour, a little at a time. Work on board, flouring if necessary. Separate into eleven pieces of dough. Roll each piece into oblong shape. Spread jam over rolled out dough. Add raisins and nuts. Sprinkle with cloves and cinnamon. Roll dough up and place on cookie sheet. Brush with water and bake at 375 degrees for fifteen minutes.

Pistachio Cookies

- 2 sticks butter
- ½ c. confectioners sugar
- 1 tsp. almond flavor
- 1½ c. flour
- 1 c. pistachio nuts, chopped
- green food coloring

Mix the preceding ingredients with a mixer. Roll out dough on a floured board into long ropes about one-inch in diameter. Cut off 1" to 1½" pieces and roll into the size of a walnut. Place on a cookie sheet. Bake at 350 degrees for ten minutes. While still warm, roll in confectioners sugar.

Variation: Use 1 teaspoon raspberry preserves and red food coloring.

COOKIE THIEF: Now we know who steals all the pignoli cookies.

Neapolitan Cookies—Rainbow Cookies

½ lb. almond paste
1 c. butter
1 c. sugar
4 egg yolks
2 c. flour
4 egg whites
1 tsp. extract
  red food coloring
  green food coloring
¼ c. raspberry jam
¼ c. apricot preserves
1 pkg (6 oz.) semi-sweet chocolate bits, melted

In a large mixing bowl, beat almond paste, butter, sugar, egg yolks, and extract until fluffy. Stir in flour. In a small bowl, beat egg whites until soft peaks form. Fold into flour mixture. Divide batter into three portions and color one green, one red, and leave one as is. Grease bottom of 13"x9" pan; line with foil and grease foil. Spread red batter. Bake at 350 degrees for eight minutes. Reline pan with foil and bake green, and then do the white. When cool, spread layer with raspberry jam and then next with apricot preserves. Set heavy object over layers and refrigerate overnight. Next day, melt chocolate and spread on cake. Let chocolate set and cut half-inch wide strips. Cut each strip into four pieces.

Mostaccioli

4½ c. flour
1½ c. sugar
1 c. honey
½ c. Crisco
1 tsp. baking soda
1 tsp. ground cinnamon
½ tsp. ground cloves
2 c. toasted almonds (you may use ½ hazelnuts)
1 egg
water, added 1 Tbsp. at a time to manage dough

Topping: Melt two boxes semi-sweet chocolate over a double-boiler.

Beat eggs, sugar, Crisco, and honey. Add cloves and cinnamon. Add some flour and toasted almonds. Add more flour and baking soda. Keep mixing and add water if necessary. Place dough on a floured board. Roll to ¼" thick and cut into diamond shapes. Bake at 350 degrees for fifteen minutes. Cool and top each cookie with melted chocolate.

Variation: Roll dough one-inch round, then slightly flatten like a bar; place on a cookie sheet. When cool, slice and coat with melted chocolate.

Boiled Taralli

        6 eggs
        1 Tbsp. sugar
        1 tsp. baking powder
        2 Tbsp. oil
           flour

Mix eggs, sugar, baking powder, and oil with mixer. Add flour slowly and as much as it will take. Place dough on a board after mixing and work well. Cover dough and let it rest for a short time. Roll dough out like a bagel. Cut all around outer edge. Boil water. When it reaches a full boil, drop in a few rolled taralli. When they rise to the top, remove and place on a cookie sheet that is lined with parchment paper. Bake at 400 degrees for thirty minutes.

Strufole

        4 c. flour
        ¼ c. oil
        2 tsp. baking powder
        1 tsp. salt
        6 jumbo eggs, beaten
        3 Tbsp. white wine

Mix ingredients and knead thoroughly into dough. Roll out with a rolling pin into a circle. With edged cutter, cut rows of dough. Cut each strip across in ½" length. Dough should end up as ½" cubes. Fry in oil, putting in handful at a time. When golden, quickly remove from pan. Drop little balls into warmed honey, coating well. Sprinkles or nuts may be added.

Italian Butter Cookies

    2¼ c. sugar
    4 c. less 1 Tbsp. shortening
    1 tsp. salt
    2 jumbo eggs plus 1 white
    1 tsp. vanilla
    5 c. less 1 Tbsp. cake flour
    1½ c. plus 2 Tbsp. regular flour
    ½ c. plus 2 Tbsp. evaporated milk

Beat sugar, shortening, and salt thoroughly. Add remaining ingredients and continue to beat till fluffy. Place dough in pastry bag with star tip. Dough may be arranged long for sandwich cookies, round like rosettes with sprinkles, Hershey's kiss, or cherry on top. Dough may be colored. Use apricot or raspberry preserves for sandwich cookies. Bake cookies at 350 degrees for fifteen minutes.

Butter Cookie with Almond Paste

    2 ¼ c. sugar
    2 c. almond paste
    1 tsp. salt
    4 c. less 1 Tbsp. shortening
    5 c. cake flour
    ½ c. plus 2 Tbsp. evaporated milk
    1 tsp. almond extract
    3 egg whites (a little over ½ c.)
    1 ½ c. plus 2 Tbsp. regular flour

Beat sugar, almond paste, salt, and shortening thoroughly. Add egg whites, flour, almond extract, and evaporated milk. Follow instructions for Italian Butter Cookie.

Torrone Cookies

    2 c. toasted, chopped hazelnuts
    2 c. toasted, chopped almonds
    3 c. sugar
    3 Tbsp. cocoa (heaping)
    5 egg whites

Mix the preceding ingredients with mixer. Roll into balls the size of a walnut. Bake at 350 degrees for fifteen minutes.

Drop Cookies

    6 jumbo eggs
    1 c. sugar
    1 c. oil
    6 tsp. baking powder
    1 Tbsp. lemon extract
  4-6 c. flour

Frosting:

    1 box confectioners sugar
    1 tsp. lemon extract
    2 Tbsp. boiling water

Mix eggs, sugar, oil, baking powder, and lemon extract. Add flour, a small amount at a time. Work dough on floured board until mixture is easy to handle. Cut dough off into several sections. With one section of dough, roll into a long length, about one-inch in diameter. Cut off into 1 ½" pieces and roll into size of a walnut. Bake at 350 degrees for fifteen minutes or until slightly golden. Frost with confectioners sugar icing.

Anisette Cookies

  2 c. eggs (about 8 eggs)
  2 c. sugar
  1 tsp. honey
  2 tsp. baking powder (level)
  6 c. flour
  1 tsp. anise oil or 1 oz. anise extract

Mix the preceding ingredients very thoroughly with mixer. Take part of the dough, and roll into a small loaf. Pat top down. Line cookie sheet with parchment paper. Bake at 350 degrees for fifteen minutes. After loaves are baked, cut diagonally and return to oven to toast sides. Check texture. *Very hard.*

Amarettini

  2 jumbo eggs
  1 c. sugar
    pinch of salt
  ¼ tsp. baking soda
  ¼ tsp. cream of tartar
  1 tsp. almond extract
  1 c. brown sugar
  ¾ c. butter
  1 c. toasted almonds, chopped
  3 c. flour
    confectioners sugar

Mix eggs, sugar, salt, baking soda, cream of tartar, brown sugar, butter, almond extract, and toasted almonds. Mix thoroughly. Add flour. Place confectioners sugar on board. Roll dough in a long roll. Cut off 1" to 1½" pieces and roll into size of walnut. Roll balls in confectioners sugar and place on cookie sheet. Bake at 350 degrees for fifteen minutes.

Pumpkin Cookies

        6 eggs
        2 c. brown sugar
        1 c. oil
        1 tsp. ground cinnamon
        1 tsp. ground cloves
        4 tsp. baking powder
        2 tsp. baking soda
        1 c. pumpkin
        1 c. shredded coconut
        1 c. chocolate chips
        2 c. chopped nuts
       4½ c. flour

Mix eggs, sugar, oil, and spices. Add flour, baking powder, baking soda, pumpkin, coconut chips, and nuts. Bake at 350 degrees for fifteen minutes.

COOKIE CRITICS: Every recipe must be thoroughly tested.

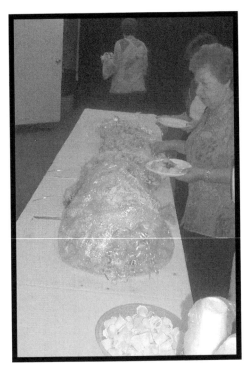

Pumpkin Squares

        1 c. shortening or butter
        4 c. brown sugar
        3 c. flour
        2 tsp. baking powder
        1 tsp. salt
        1 tsp. baking soda
        2 tsp. ground cinnamon
        2 tsp. ground cloves
        2 tsp. vanilla
        8 eggs (or 2 c.)
        2 c. pumpkin
        3 c. chopped nuts
        2 c. small M&Ms
        2 c. white and dark raisins
        1 c. orange marmalade

Beat shortening and brown sugar. Add eggs, pumpkin, spices, flour, vanilla, baking powder, and baking soda. Add raisins, nuts, and M&Ms. Grease two 9"×13" pans and flour, shaking off excess flour. Punch marmalade into batter while it's in the pan, spreading into different sections. Smooth off top of cake with hands. Bake at 350 degrees for thirty minutes.

Frosting:
        8 oz. cream cheese
        2 c. confectioners sugar
        1 tsp. vanilla
        1 tsp. marmalade
        1 stick butter

Beat ingredients thoroughly and frost cooled cake.

Sesame Cookies

    2 sticks oleo
 1½ c. sugar
    1 c. eggs
    ½ c. evaporated milk
    1 Tbsp. orange extract
 4½ c. flour
    6 tsp. baking powder
        sesame seeds

Mix oleo, sugar, eggs, milk, orange extract, flour, and baking powder. Divide dough and roll into long lengths ¾ inch thick. Roll in sesame seeds in pan. Cut into 1 ½ lengths. Cook at 350 degrees for fifteen minutes, until light brown.

Coconut Rounds

 2½ c. flour
    1 c. sugar
    2 tsp. baking powder
    ¾ c. butter
    2 Tbsp. milk
    2 tsp. vanilla
    2 eggs
    1 c. nuts, chopped
    1 c. chopped cherries
    1 c. shredded coconut

1. Mix the preceding ingredients with mixer. Place flour on table. Roll dough out. Cut in one-inch pieces. Roll in coconut.

2. May be cut into two-inch pieces. Bake and frost one end with chocolate frosting.

3. Make a long roll and slice into bars. Bake at 350 degrees for ten minutes.

Chocolate Chewies

        2 sticks butter (1 c.)
    1²/₃ c. sugar
        2 eggs
        2 c. flour
        7 Tbsp. cocoa (heaping)
           pinch of salt
        2 c. chopped nuts
      ¹/₃ c. milk
        1 tsp. vanilla
        2 tsp. baking powder
           confectioners sugar

Mix dough thoroughly. Place confectioners sugar on board. Roll dough out into ropes. Cut into one-inch pieces. Roll into size of a walnut and roll in confectioners sugar again. Bake at 350 degrees for fifteen minutes.

Pumpkin Bars

        4 eggs
    1²/₃ c. sugar
        1 c. oil
        1 can (16 oz.) pumpkin
        2 c. flour
        2 tsp. baking powder
        2 tsp. ground cinnamon
        1 tsp. salt
        1 tsp. baking soda

Beat eggs, oil, pumpkin, and sugar until light and fluffy. Mix dry ingredients. Add to pumpkin mix. Bake on an ungreased cookie sheet, 15"×10"×1", in a 350-degree oven for twenty-five minutes. Frost with Cream Cheese Frosting.

Cream Cheese Frosting:
        1 cream cheese (8 oz.)
        1 c. confectioners sugar
        1 tsp. vanilla
        4 tsp. Crisco

Pizzelle

1 dozen eggs
2 c. sugar
1 c. oil
2 tsp. baking powder
4 c. flour
anisette flavor
juice of 1 lemon
juice of 1 orange

Mix preceding ingredients thoroughly and cook on pizzelle machine.

Pistachio Butter Ball

1 c. flour
1½ c. confectioners sugar
pinch of salt
2 c. butter
4 tsp. almond extract
2 c. chopped nuts
green food coloring

Mix dough thoroughly. Roll dough in a 1 ½″ long rope. Cut off one-inch pieces and roll into size of a walnut. Bake at 350 degrees for ten minutes. Roll in confectioners sugar while warm.

Peanut Butter Balls

½ c. Crisco
1½ c. peanut butter
1 tsp. vanilla
16 oz. confectioners sugar

Combine all ingredients till smooth. Add drop of water if necessary. Roll into balls, put on wax paper on cookie sheet, and refrigerate for one hour—or refrigerate as is for one hour and then roll into balls.

In a double boiler, add two tablespoons Crisco and six ounces chocolate chips; melt. Use a toothpick and stab peanut butter ball; dip in chocolate and place on wax paper. Chill. Place in plastic bag and stick in the refrigerator.

Almond Cup

2 c. flour
¼ tsp. salt
½ c. sugar
½ c. oleo
1 egg
1 tsp. vanilla

Mix the preceding ingredients thoroughly. Roll dough out and, using a cookie cutter, line small cupcake tins with dough.

Filling:
1 egg
¼ c. sugar
½ tsp. almond extract
½ c. almond paste
1 egg (whole)

Mix together till creamy. Place one teaspoon in each cup. Bake cupcakes at 350 degrees for twenty-five minutes.

Bow Cookie

- ¼ lb. butter
- ⅓ c. oil
- 1 c. sugar
- 6 beaten eggs
- pinch of salt
- 2 tsp. extract
- 5 c. flour
- 4 Tbsp. baking powder

Blend butter, oil, and sugar; cream well. Add eggs and extract. Sift flour, baking powder, and salt. Mix into batter. Pinch off small pieces, about a tablespoon, and roll to thickness of pencil. Form into figure eights. Bake on an ungreased cookie sheet for twelve to fifteen minutes at 400 degrees.

Chocolate Covered Cherry Cookies

    3 c. flour
    1 c. cocoa
    ½ tsp. salt
    ½ tsp. baking powder
    ½ tsp. baking soda
    2 semi-sweet chocolate bits (6 oz.)
    1 c. sweetened condensed milk
    1 c. Crisco
    2 c. sugar
    2 eggs
    3 tsp. vanilla
    2 jars maraschino cherries (10 oz.)

In a large bowl, stir together flour, cocoa, salt, baking powder, and soda. In mixer bowl, beat together oleo and sugar at low speed till fluffy. Add eggs and vanilla; beat well. Gradually add dry ingredients to creamed mixture. Beat till well blended. Shape dough into one-inch balls and place on an ungreased cookie sheet. Press down center of dough with thumb. Drain maraschino cherries, reserving juice. Place a cherry in the center of each cookie. Bake at 350 degrees for ten minutes.

In a small saucepan, combine chocolate pieces and sweetened condensed milk. Heat till chocolate melts. Stir in eight teaspoons reserved cherry juice. Spoon about one teaspoon frosting over each cherry, spreading to cover cherry.

Cherry Winks

   4½ c. flour
    2 tsp. baking powder
    1 tsp. salt
    1 tsp. soda
  1½   c. shortening
    2 c. sugar
    1 c. cherries
    4 eggs
    4 Tbsp. milk
    2 tsp. vanilla
    1 pkg. dates, chopped
    1 c. nuts, chopped
    4 c. crushed corn flakes

Mix flour, baking powder, soda, and salt. Blend butter and sugar. Add eggs and beat. Stir in milk and vanilla. Add nuts, dates, and two-thirds cup finely chopped cherries. Mix. Shape dough into balls, then roll in crushed corn flakes. Press cherry in center of rolled dough. Bake at 350 degrees for ten to twelve minutes.

Chocolate Chip Cookies

6¾ flour
3 tsp. baking powder
½ tsp. baking soda
3 tsp. salt
3 c. butter, softened
2¼ c. sugar
2¼ c. brown sugar
3 tsp. vanilla extract
6 eggs
3 pkg. (12 oz.) chocolate chips
3. c. chopped nuts

In a small bowl, combine flour, baking soda, and salt; set aside. In a large bowl, combine butter, sugar, brown sugar, and vanilla extract. Beat until creamy. Beat in eggs. Gradually add flour mixture. Stir in chocolate chips and nuts. Drop by rounded teaspoon on an ungreased cookie sheet. Bake at 375 degrees for eight to ten minutes.

Butter Ball

2 c. butter
8 tsp. powdered sugar
2 tsp. vanilla
4 c. flour
2 c. chopped nuts

Cream butter. Add sugar and continue to beat until light. Add vanilla flavor and flour; fold in nuts. Shape into small balls. Place on an ungreased cookie sheet. Bake at 350 degrees for fifteen to eighteen minutes. Roll in confectioners sugar while hot.

Butterhorn Cookies

2 c. flour
½ c. oleo
1 egg
¾ c. sour cream

Mix all preceding ingredients. Shape into a ball. Sprinkle with flour and wrap in wax paper. Refrigerate for two hours. Divide dough into three sections. Roll one portion into a large circle one-eighth inch thick.

Mix:

¾ c. sugar
1 tsp. cinnamon
¾ c. chopped nuts

Spread preceding ingredients on pie-shaped dough. Cut into pie wedges. Roll from large end to smaller end. Bake at 375 degrees for twenty-five to thirty-five minutes.

Biscotti

½ c. toasted almonds
1 c. butter
1½ c. sugar
4 eggs
1 tsp. amaretto
1 Tbsp. baking soda
½ tsp. salt
4¼ c. flour

Cream butter and sugar. Add dry ingredients. Add eggs, one at a time, to mixture. Mix slivered almonds into the dough for a brief period of time, six to seven seconds when using an electric mixer. Shape the dough into a loaf and place on baking sheet that is either covered with parchment paper or is greased. Bake at 325 degrees until golden brown. Cut while hot, slanting knife at an angle for a bias cut. Bake at 325 degrees for thirty minutes.

Dolce Cookie

> 6 eggs
> 2 c. sugar
> 3 tsp. baking powder
> 1 c. oleo
> ½ c. milk
> 2 tsp. orange extract
> 5 c. flour

Beat sugar, eggs, and oleo; cream well. Add dry ingredients alternately with milk. Add orange extract. Sprinkle board with confectioners sugar and roll a long rope 1 ½ inches wide. Cut off one-inch pieces and roll in confectioners sugar. Bake at 350 degrees for ten minutes.

POOF! If company came to the house, out of nowhere cookies would appear.

Italian Christmas Chocolate Drops

  8 c. flour
  2 tsp. baking powder
  1 tsp. baking soda
  ¼ tsp. salt
  4 c. sugar
  1 c. plus 4 Tbsp. Crisco
  1 c. less 4 Tbsp. cocoa
12 oz. chocolate chips
  1 tsp. ground cinnamon
  1 tsp. ground cloves
  ¼ tsp. black pepper
  4 oz. whiskey
  2 c. milk
  1 c. nuts

Mix ingredients together. Drop by teaspoon on a greased and floured cookie sheet. Bake at 375 degrees for fifteen minutes. While warm, dip quickly into thick frosting.

Frosting:
  4 c. confectioners sugar
  ½ c. oleo
  ½ c. milk

Italian Chocolate Cookies

8 c. flour
1 c. shortening
2 c. sugar
1 c. raisins, chopped
½ Tbsp. ground allspice
1 c. nuts, chopped
3 Tbsp. cocoa
½ c. orange juice
1 c. warm water
2 Tbsp. baking powder

Add shortening to warm water, then add orange juice and sugar. Mix with rest of ingredients. Fold in raisins and nuts last. Dough will be stiff. Form into size of walnuts and bake at 350 degrees on a lightly greased cookie sheet for fifteen to twenty minutes.

Frosting:

3 c. confectioners sugar
4 tsp. light corn syrup
1 Tbsp. liqueur
¼ c. hot water
⅛ tsp. salt

Add water, a little at a time, for desired consistency.

Italian Do Do Cookies

    8 c. flour
    2 c. sugar
       shredded coconut
    1 c. Hershey's cocoa
    2 tsp. ground cinnamon
    2 tsp. ground cloves
    3 tsp. baking powder
    1 c. melted shortening
    2 c. cooked coffee
    ½ lb. walnuts, chopped
    ½ box raisins, chopped
    ½ can applesauce
       vanilla

Mix dry ingredients together. Place raisins in coffee to soak for a short time. Add coffee, raisins, and applesauce to dry ingredients. Roll into round balls, and place on a lightly greased cookie sheet. Bake at 350 degrees for twelve to fifteen minutes.

CHAPTER TEN
Food and friends

After I opened my restaurant in Bristol, I made some great friends. Ten years later and several miles removed, these guys are still great friends. Over the years, hanging out with Elliot, Bam, and Nice-Guy Bob has produced some terrific stories.

The Guy that Ate Three Full Meals at My Restaurant

One of the gentlemen named above once set up three dates for a Friday night. I won't mention any names, but Bob is too nice of a guy to arrange three dates for the same night and Bam is married. So Elliot says to me, "You know how it is, you have to have a back up in case one or two of your dates flakes out on you, and one or two always flakes out." Well, not this night. His evening started at four in the afternoon. His first date walks in, and we sit them in a booth. They don't get menus—none of my friends do. They just eat what I put in front of them. "Franco," he says to me, "we would like to eat light." In other words, "I have to eat three times tonight, so take it easy on me. " Now being the good friend that I am, I gave him the biggest heaviest dish I could cook. I made gnocchi with a four-cheese cream sauce. Our nickname for this dish is "belly bombs" because they are so good you can't stop eating them but, boy, do they sit in your gut. Oh, by the way, the gnocchi is just the first course. After that came the veal marsala, which is his favorite dish. Even with his game plan, I know he can't pass up the opportunity to eat the whole thing. Then I bring them dessert. They eat, they drink a little, they kiss and say good night.

After the first date leaves, we reset the same table and he sits down again. Before his date arrives, he takes me aside and begs me. "Franco, please, please be nice and send out some light food, maybe just some apps." His second date arrives, sits down, and I walk out, and say, "Hello, hope your hungry."

"I'm starving," she says. Elliot rolls his eyes in the back of his head, thinking to himself, here we go again. I send out broccoli rabe with sausage and hot peppers, then penne ala vodka, and finally cannoli. Not a bad meal—if it's the only one you're eating. They finish a bottle of wine, and she leaves.

Now his next date is already sitting at the bar. Elliot pops two Tums and greets her. Again, we sit them at the same table. I come out, and with a smirk on my face I say, "Hello, I hope you're hungry."

To my disappointment, she says, "I hope you don't mind, but I already ate. Maybe we can have coffee and dessert." You should have seen the look of relief on Elliott's face.

NICE-GUY BOB AND ELLIOT: After I opened my restaurant in Bristol, I made some great friends. Hanging out with these guys has produced some great stories.

MENU
for Heavy Dates

Gnocchi with Quarto Fromage Cream Sauce
Veal Marsala
Broccoli Rabe with Sausage and Hot Peppers
Penne ala Vodka
Cannoli

Gnocchi with Quarto Fromage Cream Sauce

- 2 c. heavy cream
- ¼ lb. butter
- ½ c. parmesan cheese
- ½ c. mozzarella cheese
- ½ c. gorgonzola cheese
- ½ c. romano cheese
- 1 lb. cooked gnocchi pasta
- chopped parsley

In a pan reduce cream and butter. Add all of your cheeses, mix, toss in pasta, and serve.

Veal Marsala

- 4 veal scaloppini
- 10 mushrooms sliced
- ¼ c. marsala wine
- flour
- oil for sautéing
- 1 c. brown sauce
- 2 Tbsp. butter
- salt and pepper

Heat oil in a large sauté pan. Coat veal with flour, and place in oil. Sauté till brown. Flip. Add mushrooms— sauté. Drain oil Add wine, and reduce sauce. Add brown sauce. Add butter. Reduce till thick, and serve.

Broccoli Rabe with Sausage and Hot Peppers
    1 lb. spicy Italian sausage links
    6 cherry peppers, cut in half
    1 lb. cooked broccoli rabe
    3 cloves garlic, chopped
       olive oil

Heat olive oil in a pan. Add sausage and sauté until golden brown. Put in a 350-degree oven for ten minutes. Remove from oven. Add garlic and peppers to the hot pan, and sauté. Then add cooked broccoli rabe. Serve with fresh olive oil drizzled over the top.

Penne ala Vodka
    ½ lb. cooked penne pasta
    1 oz. Vodka
    1 small red onion, chopped
    ¼ lb. proscuitto
    2 c. tomato sauce
    1 c. cream
    1 c. parmigiano cheese

In a large pan, sauté prosciutto and onions. Deglaze with vodka. Add tomato sauce and cream. Bring to a simmer and reduce sauce. Add pasta and toss in cheese.

ôôô

Closing Out the Weekend

Nice-Guy Bob got his nickname only because he used to hang out with us. In fact, compared to Elliot. Bam, and me he should have been called "Saint Bob." Well, every Sunday, Nice-Guy Bob, Elliot, Bam, me, and a couple of other guys would sit down to a family dinner at the restaurant, nurse our hangovers, eat, and b.s. about the weekend. A typical menu looked like this:

MENU
Closing Out the Weekend Menu

Pasta e Fagioli Soup
Steak Pizzaiola
Spumoni

Pasta e Fagioli Soup

¼ lb. cannelloni beans (raw)
¼ lb. red kidney beans (raw)
15 c. water
1 c. chopped celery
1 onion, chopped
¼ c. olive oil
5 peeled tomatoes
½ lb. tubettini pasta
    salt and pepper to taste

Combine water, onion, celery, tomatoes, and beans. Boil approximately one hour until beans are tender. Add oil and pasta. Boil until pasta is tender. Season with salt and pepper. Serve hot.

Steak Pizzaiola

    3 chuck fillet steaks
    1 pepperoncino (hot), chopped
    1 tsp. chopped oregano
    2 cloves garlic, minced
    1 Tbsp. chopped basil
    1 can crushed tomatoes
  ⅓ c. olive oil
  ½ c. grated cheese

In a deep pan, combine oil, garlic, and steaks. Fry steaks until brown. Add tomatoes, pepper, oregano, pepperoncino, and basil. Bring to boil. If sauce is too thick, add one cup water. Simmer over medium heat for approximately one hour. Serve over pasta, and top with grated cheese.

Spumoni

    1 c. vanilla ice cream
    1 c. strawberry ice cream
    1 c. pistachio ice cream
  ⅓ c. chopped maraschino cherries
    1 c. sliced almonds

Place all ingredients in a mixer. Blend until mixed together. Place in a mold and freeze.

                        ☙☙☙

Freakin' Bob

Wherever we went, when the server asked what we would like for desert, Bob says, "Do you have spumoni?" Well, here you are Mr. Nice Guy, now you can make your own.

అఅఅ

Bam! Wrong Pasta!

Now Bam grew up in the restaurant business, so you'd think he would know his way around a kitchen. Once Bam was sitting at the bar and the cook called in sick, so I asked Bam for help. Boy, was that a mistake. I kept telling him what pasta I needed, and we had at least six different shaped pastas in the kitchen. When it was time to put the pasta with the sauce, he put all of the different pastas in the same pan and we had to start all over again. This backed us up so much that we sent Nice-Guy Bob out to talk to the tables and tell them their dinner would take a couple minutes longer. Boy, that Bob, he sure is a Nice Guy.

CHAPTER ELEVEN

Food Is Passion

Rule # 1: Cook What You Like

Okay, think about cooking as a way to express your passion. Don't think of it as a choir. As I tell people who sit through one of my cooking classes, cook what you enjoy cooking. For example, suppose you decide to throw a dinner party for your neighbors and they tell you they love red snapper. Well, what you really wanted to cook was salmon, but you try to please them by making red snapper. Stop that! It's a mistake. Cook what you like. Make the salmon. Not only will you enjoy making it, you will put your passion into it. Let's face it, folks are more passionate about what they like to do than what they have to do. If your neighbors like red snapper, let them cook it for you when you go to their house.

Rule # 2: Use All Five Senses

Cooking is the only job where you use all five senses:

See—You look at the food and see it in all its beauty.

Touch—You feel the texture and freshness of the food.

Smell—You love to smell the food before it's cooked, while it's being cooked, and afterwards, when it is on your plate.

Hear—You listen to food while it's cooking—listen to the crackle of the oil while its sautéing—and as you eat it. Crunch.

Taste—This one is self explanatory, and you hope it tastes as good as looks, feels, smells, and sounds.

Rule #3: Surprise Yourself

Okay, back to the passion of food. Sometimes things work out better when you don't have a plan. Don't be afraid to take some of the recipes in this book and embellish on them. You might look at a dish like the fried peppers and potatoes in chapter three and say, "Hey, that would be great served over pork chops instead of a side dish."

On that note, people often ask me how I create the unique dishes on my menu. Well, it is three simple things that I look for in a dish: flavor, texture, surprise.

Flavor—Be smart. You don't want make ice cream out of salmon. You already have an idea in your head about which foods might work together. Experiment. Start with little things, like adding sun-dried tomatoes to your favorite chicken dish. See where this takes the flavor profile of that dish.

Texture—When you bite into a dish like Veal Tusciano, you get the roughness of sautéed veal, the firmness of the mushrooms, the smoothness of the cream.

FRANCO'S RULE #1: Cook what you like. Let's face it, folks are more passionate about what they want to do than what they have to do.

Surprise—this is a little hard to explain. Let's take that Veal Tusciano. When you eat it the basic recipe, you get a nice smoothness from the cream sauce. If you add sun-dried tomatoes, you get a little tart explosion in your mouth. Then the mushroom smooths it out. If you add artichoke hearts, you get another little explosion and so on. Surprise.

Here is another trick. Buy huge serving dishes. When you serve family style, these serving dishes make an awesome statement

These next recipes are what I like to call "Franco P Originals."

Fried Pasta Napoleon

Pasta Dough:
> 1 c. eggs
> 1 c. water
> 4 c. flour

Knead dough. Cut into six pieces and roll through pasta machine. Cut into triangles and fry.

Filling:
> 1 lb. ricotta cheese
> 1 c. diced roasted peppers
> 1 small red onion, minced
> 2 Tbsp. gorgonzola cheese
> salt and pepper

Mix all ingredients together and spoon on the fried pasta. Stack three high.

Sauce:
> 4 oz. Boursin cheese
> 2 Tbsp. cream

Mix together for the sauce.

Pumpkin Tiramisu

- 1 lb. mascarpone cheese
- 5 eggs, separated
- ⅔ c. sugar
- 1 pkg. lady fingers
- ¼ c. coffee liquor
- 1 c. espresso
- 1 can pumpkin
  ground all spice
  ground cinnamon

In a medium bowl, beat egg yolks with a wire whisk until frothy. Beat in sugar and mascarpone. In another bowl, whip egg whites until stiff. In another bowl, mix pumpkin, all spice, and cinnamon. Then blend pumpkin and mascarpone mixes. Fold in the egg whites. Dip lady fingers in coffee and place on a serving dish. Place some pumpkin mixture on top, then another layer of lady fingers, then more of the pumpkin mixture.

Veal con Porcini

- 4 veal medallions pounded
  flour
  salt
  pepper
  cognac
- ½ c. brown sauce
- 3 oz. dried porcini mushrooms soaked
- 2 oz. heavy cream
- 1 Tbsp. butter

Coat veal with flour, and sauté till golden brown. Flame with cognac. Add mushrooms, brown sauce, cream, and butter. Reduce sauce and serve.

Grana Padano Napoleons
with fresh mozzarella and tomatoes

Grana Padano Crisps:
- 2 oz. grana padano cheese (shredded)
- 3 tsp. butter

In a non-stick pan, melt one teaspoon butter. Place one-half ounce of cheese into pan and shake into a circle. Cook until golden brown. Flip with a rubber spatula. When the other side is golden brown, slide onto a paper towel and pat dry with another towel. Repeat this process two more times with the remaining cheese.

Napoleons:
- 3 oz. roasted red peppers
- 1 beefsteak tomato, sliced
- 4 oz. fresh mozzarella
- 5 fresh basil leaves
  - salt
  - black pepper grinder
  - extra virgin olive oil

When crisps are dry, place in the center of a ten-inch plate. Slice the tomato and place on top of the crisp covering the entire crisp. Salt and pepper the tomatoes, then place another crisp on top of the tomato. Slice the mozzarella into five slices, and save a slice for garnish. Place the remaining four slices over the Grana Padano Crisp. Drizzle olive oil over the cheese, and salt and pepper. Cover the cheese with the remaining crisp. In the center of crisp, place one slice of tomato, one slice of fresh mozzarella, and two basil leaves. Cut the red pepper into three triangles and arrange on the plate at 12, 4, and 9 o'clock. Then place the other three basil leaves between them. Drizzle olive oil over the entire plate and serve.

Ice Cream Burrito

½ gal. vanilla ice cream
3 tortilla shells
2 papayas
1 mango
 butter
½ c. sugar
 chocolate sauce
 diced nuts

Peel and chop the mangos and papayas. Place in a pan with butter and heat. Add sugar and remove from the heat. Place ice cream in a tortilla shell and wrap like a burrito. Cover with chocolate sauce and nuts. Add stewed fruit.

Chicken With Spinach and Portabella Mushrooms

4 each 6 oz. chicken breast
1 lb. spinach
4 each portabella mushrooms
1 small red onion
 olive oil
 sliced mozzarella cheese
1 can chicken stock
 garlic
 salt and pepper
 flour
¼ stick butter

In a sauté pan, heat oil. When oil is hot, dredge the chicken in flour and sauté. Slice the onions and mushrooms, and add to the pan. Then add garlic and half can of chicken stock Add salt and pepper and butter, and reduce. In another pan, heat remaining chicken stock. Add spinach and cook. Place spinach on a plate, place the chicken on top of spinach, and top with sauce and mozzarella.

Shrimp Luciano

 6 jumbo shrimp, peeled
 3 eggs, beaten
   flour
 3 slices prociutto ham, cut in half
 6 slices fresh mozzarella cheese
 2 Tbsp. butter
   juice of 1 lemon
 ½ c. sherry wine
 ⅓ c. olive oil
   salt and pepper

Heat olive oil in a pan. Dredge shrimp in flour, then in egg. Sauté shrimp in hot oil. Flip and sauté for another minute. Top with ham and cheese. Add butter, lemon juice, and wine. Reduce sauce. Add salt and pepper to taste.

CHAPTER TWELVE

Paravicini's Italian Bistro

How to Choose a Name

Paravicini can be loosely translated as "for the neighbors." With that in mind, my partner and I tried with some success to make Paravicini's the neighborhood Italian restaurant on the West Side of Colorado Springs.

But Paravicini has a more important meaning. Paravicini is the maiden name of Beatrice (Paravicini) Sexton, my partner's mother. We chose the name not only because of its Italian to English translation but to pay homage to Mrs. Paravicini Sexton. We agree that we have a perfect name.

The Food, the Wine, and the Passion

We have found our niche. Paravicini's Italian Bistro has every thing you would expect from a neighborhood Italian restaurant—and a few surprises. Maybe that's why we were voted the best new restaurant in 2004 by the *Colorado Springs Gazette*. I have always been proud of the food that I have put out for my family, friends, and customers over the years. At Paravicini's, though, I went back to basics. I put all of the trends aside and stick to old-fashioned southern Italian peasant food. Today I am putting out the greatest food of my career. Now I prepare Chicken Valeria, Shrimp Paravicini, and Tiramisu according to traditional recipes. I take tradition seriously. My Mom flew out to Colorado to make sure my sous chef, Creg Carson, was making our Tiramisu the same way she would. We priced the menu so that you don't have to take out a loan to eat here. The atmosphere is warm and casual; the wine list is priced modestly (no bottle costs more than $30.00); the service staff is friendly and knowledgeable. It is not any one of these things that makes a great restaurant but all of them put together.

Chicken Valeria

    2 chicken breasts
    1 Tbsp. minced garlic
    1 oz. sun dried tomatoes, chopped
    1 oz. artichoke hearts. chopped
    1 oz. mushrooms, sliced
    4 fl. oz. brown sauce
    2 oz. wine
    1 oz. butter
       olive oil
       salt pepper
       flour

Heat oil in pan. Coat chicken with flour. Place chicken in hot oil. Sauté on both sides until golden brown. Add garlic, sun-dried tomatoes, artichoke hearts, and mushrooms. Deglaze pan with white wine. Add brown sauce. Salt and pepper. Finish with butter.

TED AND FRANCO: Paravicini can be loosely translated as "for the neighbors." With that in mind, my partner and I tried to make Paravicini's the neighborhood Italian restaurant on the West Side of Colorado Springs. But it has a more important meaning ...

Shrimp Paravicini

   1 Tbsp. olive oil
   ¾ lb. medium shrimp, peeled and deveined
   ½ c. chopped tomatoes
   ¼ c. dry white wine
   1 clove garlic, thinly sliced
     salt and pepper
   ¼ c. fresh basil
   1 small onion, diced
   ¼ c. cream
   1 piece toasted Italian bread per serving

Heat oil in a medium frying pan over medium heat. Add shrimp and cook, stirring, just until shrimp begin to curl and turn pink (about one minute). Add onions, tomatoes, white wine, and garlic. Increase heat to high, and cook, stirring until shrimp are just opaque through (one to two minutes longer. Add cream and reduce. Serve over Italian bread.

Tiramisu

1 lb. mascarpone cheese
5 eggs, separated
⅔ c. sugar
1 pkg. lady fingers
¼ c. coffee liqueur
1 pint espresso
1 chocolate bar

In a medium bowl, beat egg yolks with a wire whisk until frothy. Add sugar and mascarpone, and continue to mix. In another bowl, whip egg whites until stiff. Fold egg whites into the mascarpone mix. In a separate container, mix espresso and liquor together. Dip lady fingers one at a time into the coffee liqueur, and place into a serving dish. When bottom is covered with lady fingers, place mascarpone mixture on top. Then add another layer of lady fingers and another layer of mascarpone mixture. Shave chocolate over the top, and let sit for at least six hours.

ॐॐॐ

A Few Surprises

Even though Paravicini's emphasizes tradition, we try to surprise our guests with cooking classes, nightly dinner specials, and theme dinners. Our most popular theme has been the "BIG NIGHT DINNER." In the movie, *The Big Night*, Primo and Secondo are two brothers who emigrate from Italy and open an Italian restaurant in America. Primo (Franco) is the irascible and gifted chef, brilliant in his culinary genius but determined not to squander his talent on making routine dishes that customers expect. Secondo (Ted) is the smooth front-man, trying to keep the restaurant financially afloat even though they have few patrons other than a poor artist who pays with his paintings. The owner of the nearby Pascal's restaurant (similar to a chain restaurant that is enormously successful in spite of its mediocre fare) offers a solution—he will call his friend, a big-time jazz musician, to play a special benefit at the brothers' restaurant. Primo begins to prepare his masterpiece, a feast of a lifetime, for the brothers' big night ...

Okay, first of all, we are not desperately trying to keep the restaurant afloat; Franco isn't that much of a genius; and Ted certainly isn't that smooth. Nevertheless, at the BIG NIGHT DINNER is our homage to the movie. The food is plentiful, the wine does flows, and the musician does show up! It is always a great night of food and friendship. Below are the recipes.

Roasted Portabella and Pepper Salad with Goat Cheese

    3 oz. romaine lettuce
    1 portabella mushroom roasted in oven
    2 oz. roasted red pepper
    2 oz. goat cheese
       olive oil
       salt and pepper

Chop romaine and place in a dish. Slice mushrooms and peppers, and arrange on top. Sprinkle goat cheese on top. Drizzle with olive oil, and finish with salt and pepper

Veal Angelo

6 oz. veal pounded thin
4 each artichoke hearts
½ c. mushrooms
2 oz. sun-dried tomatoes
1 tsp. Dijon mustard
½ c. veal stock
olive oil

Sauté veal in olive oil. Add artichoke hearts, mushrooms, sun-dried tomatoes, Dijon mustard, and veal stock. Let simmer and serve.

Calamari Arrabiatta

1 oz. olive oil
8 oz. calamari
2 oz. hot cherry peppers
1 oz. Italian black olives
1 oz. sun-dried tomatoes
1 oz. garlic
2 oz. tomato sauce
½ oz. wine
½ lb. cooked pasta

Heat olive oil in a sauté pan. Sauté calamari. Add hot cherry peppers, Italian black olives, sun-dried tomatoes, and garlic. Hit with wine, and add tomato sauce. Serve over pasta.

Timbello

The Dough:

- 4 c. flour
- 2 tsp. salt
- 2 oz. yeast
- 1 c. water

In a two-quart stainless steel mixing bowl, mix all ingredients together. Cover with a cloth and let sit for one hour. Flatten dough, then allow to rise another thirty minutes. Roll the dough flat, then fit into oven-proof dish.

The Filling:

- 1 lb. cooked penne pasta
- 3 oz. ground romano cheese
- 6 oz. shredded mozzarella
- 4 3-oz. cooked meatballs (cut into quarters)
- 8 1-oz. ground spicy Italian sausage (roll into 1 oz. balls and pre-cook)
- 4 hard-boiled eggs (cut into quarters)
- 12 oz. marinara sauce

Spray bowl with non-stick spray and dust with flour Mix all filling ingredients together. Fill to top of dough-lined bowl. Cover the top of bowl by folding over the dough. Bake in a 375-degree oven until golden brown (about thirty minutes with an internal temperature of 160 degrees). Place a cutting board over the bowl, and turn it over.

I Can't Think of a Better Way to Grow Up

Traditions. Every ethnic group has them. The different customs that immigrants brought with them to this country now make up American culture. The richness and diversity of these traditions is what makes America great. My brother, my sister, and I were lucky that our parents instilled traditions in us, traditions that we that we can now pass on to our kids. Italians came to this country and migrated into little neighborhoods. In the neighborhood where I grew up—Town Plot in Waterbury, Connecticut, every one knew whose kid you were. This was (mostly) a good thing. You could go to the deli and get a sandwich with no money, and the owners would get it from your mom later. You felt safe walking down the street and leaving your doors unlocked. A good neighborhood was all about honor and respect, and what an honor it was for me to grow up in a first generation Italian-American neighborhood.

La Famiglia
My aunts and uncles all lived within walking distance of our house. Food was never more than ten

minutes away. If I was hungry, I could always visit one of my relatives. I never had to ask. I just showed up at Aunt Rose's, Aunt Betty's, or Aunt Eleanor's house. The food always came. Summer time was the best because they all had gardens. Uncle Frank had the biggest. He had everything—tomatoes, onions, cucumbers, lettuce, green beans. Uncle Vinny Orlando was always good for a soda. My mom never bought soda because someone told her it rots your stomach. Uncle Vinny Cinquegrana hooked me on banana splits. I would help him around the yard, and he would take me to Carvel for a banana split. I think he liked banana splits better than I did, but I was his excuse to get one. My brother Joe loves to cook, and he thinks he cooks better then I do (Joe, fuhgetaboutit, but he is a great cook). My sister Gina, on the other hand, did not receive the culinary genes. Her greatest culinary achievement is macaroni and cheese with cut up hot dogs, but she is a great artist. The three of us will pass the Pisani traditions to our children. My mother taught my wife, Michele, how to make the red sauce, and the last time my mother visited she taught my daughter, Gabriela, how to make home-made pasta. I don't know which of my two children, Antonio or Gabriella, will become the next great cook in the family, but there is Mary Pisani blood in there veins and I'm sure one of them will be.

INFLUENCES: Thanks to la famiglia, my brother, my sister, and I will pass on the Pisani traditions to our children.

Bonus Recipes

Summer-time Salad from Uncle Frank's Garden

        6   tomatoes
        2   cucumbers
        1   large onion
        2   cloves garlic
            salt and pepper
        1   tsp. crushed red pepper
        6   leaves fresh basil
        ¼   cup olive oil

Mix all ingredients in a large bowl and serve with hot Italian bread.

Italian Cream Soda

    1 ½   oz. flavored syrup
        5   oz. soda water
    1 ½   oz. Half-and-Half
            ice

Fill a glass with ice. Add syrup. Fill glass with soda water , one inch from the top. Float Half-and-Half on top.

Uncle Vinny's Banana Split

        1   banana
        3   scoops vanilla ice cream
        2   oz. chocolate sauce
        2   oz. strawberries in syrup
        2   Tbsp. chopped walnuts
            whipped cream
            maraschino cherry

Peel and split banana. Place one on each side of the dish. Place ice cream in the middle. Pour chocolate sauce on one half and strawberry sauce on the other. Sprinkle with nuts. Top with whipped cream and a cherry.

Joe Pisani's Tutto de Mare

        12 clams,
        12 shrimp
         2 lbs. calamari,
        12 mussels
         1 can scungili
         2 cans crushed tomatoes
         2 cloves garlic
        ¼ c. olive oil
       2½ c. water
         6 leaves fresh basil
         1 lb. cooked linguini
            salt and pepper

Sauté clams and mussels in olive oil. Add calamari, shrimp, and scungili. Add garlic, tomatoes, and water. Simmer until all clams and mussels are open. Add fresh basil and salt and pepper. Serve over pasta.

CONTINUING THE TRADITION: Who will be the next chef in the family?

Alphabetical Index of Recipes

Made in the USA
San Bernardino, CA
19 November 2013